DAMN, DAMN, DAMN!

My Vision Board Doesn't Work

Certified Vision Board Instructor

TAWAWN LOWE

Published by TLC Publishing

Copyright@2019

All rights are reserved. No part of this book shall be reproduced or transmitted in any form or by any means, electronic or mechanical, including photocopying, recording or by any information storage and retrieval system without written permission of the publisher, excerpt for inclusion of brief quotation in a review.

Printed in the United States
Tawawn Lowe
DAMN, DAMN, DAMN!
My Vision Board Don't Work
978-0-9788090-7-2

Library of Congress Number
2019901102

Disclaimer

The purpose of this book is to educate. The author or publisher does not guarantee that anyone following the techniques, suggestions, tips, ideas or strategies will become successful. The author and publisher shall have neither liability or responsibility to anyone with respect to any loss or damaged caused, or alleged to be caused, directly or indirectly by information contained in this book.

DREAM
A dream written with a date becomes a

GOAL
A goal broken down into steps becomes a

PLAN
A plan backed by

ACTION
Makes your dreams

REALITY

Table of Contents

*****

INTRODUCTION 1
   Now Let's Talk About Vision Boards...... 5

CHAPTER 1: SELF LIMITING BELIEFS 13
   How to identify a Limiting Belief 16
   Replacing the Self-Limiting Belief with Limitless Believing 19
   If all else fails, try "if" 25

CHAPTER 2: WHAT ARE THE STORIES YOU ARE TELLING YOURSELF – ABOUT YOURSELF 27
   Understand Your Stories 30
   Tell Yourself a Different Fairy Tale 32
   Getting the Help, You Need 34
   Surround Yourself with Equals 35

CHAPTER 3: NEVER WISH HARDER THAN YOU ARE PREPARED TO WORK 39
   Take the Small First Steps 43
   Being Scared of Failing 45
   Remove Toxicity 47
   Enthusiasm 51
   Leave blank spaces 52

Always leave black spaces on your board. Intentionally..52
Finally ... .54

ABOUT THE AUTHOR..........................**59**

INTRODUCTION

I must tell you that I love all things vision boards. I believe every person should have a vision for their life, and a vision board that depicts their dreams and goals. Vision boards are an excellent visualization tool to help you get your dreams and aspirations on paper, keep your focus on the things that are important to you, remind you of your "why", inspire and motivate when you lose faith of the vision you have for your life.

I will never forget the first time I created a vision board. I was navigating my second divorce, and my primary goal was to be better, and not bitter. I remember reading the book "The Secret", and how so many of the concepts resonated with me. "The Secret was my first introduction to the concepts of vision boards, the art of allowing, and the law of attraction. Being a control freak learning about the art of allowing was intriguing, and creating a vision board tapped into my creative side. The book opened my mind to new perspectives and gave me another way of approaching this major life changing transitions. In 2009, I created my first vision board, and from that point they became a fundamental part of my personal, spiritual, professional growth and development. Did I mention, I also use vision boards with my corporate and individual clients. Vision boards is an excellent tool for helping leaders communicate their vision, team building, picture goal setting, and getting clarity on your dreams and aspirations.

Now my first vision board wasn't like the traditional vision boards they talked about in "The Secret". It didn't have pictures of cars, houses, trips, or material things. It was a picture of a heart with two words "bitter and better". I called it a healing/mindset board.

For about 6-months, I looked at my vision board every day, recited positive affirmations and scriptures, practiced the art of allowing, showed gratitude (even towards my ex-husband), prayed and asked the universe to help me feel better. Now I really didn't ask the universe to help me feel better, but I did ask the creator of the universe - God. I figured since He created the universe, He could definitely heal my broken heart. I can honestly say I didn't feel bitter, but I didn't feel better, I didn't feel anything. So of course, like most people who don't think their vision board is working, I found my self-asking that same question - Why is my vision board not working? One night while sitting on the side of my bed I looked over at my vision board laying upside down on the floor, I picked it up, stared at it for just a couple minutes, and the light bulb came on. The reasons I was not manifesting change I desired was revealed.

My name is Tawawn, I am a certified life coach and one of 150 certified vision board coaches globally, and I am passionate about helping individuals maximize their potential to become their best self, and create their best life. Through my business TL Consultancy, I use the vision board concept to assist organizations with communicating their vision and objectives, team building, leadership development, and other talent management objectives; and to teach individuals how to use combine creative visualization and a vision board as a success tool to bring forth change, and transformation, healing, problem solving, and become innovative.

I created the Envision Your Future: The Vision Board Experience (VBE) Masterclass to teach the masses on how to use a vision board as success tool. The (VBE) curriculum model has been tested and proven to be a powerful tool to bring forth personally and professionally change, and transformation. The VBE has been presented in the marketplace, and to organizations, ministries, small business, and committed individuals like you who want change, or to achieve a higher level of success.

As a leading expert on vision boards, I want to help you make a vision board that will turn your dreams into reality. Teaching you how to use a vision board as a success tool is only a small part of my coaching goals. Helping you understand the concept of the vision board, the power of visualization, the mistakes in using a vision, and why vision boards don't work for some is even a bigger part of my responsibilities to you.

Now Let's Talk About Vision Boards……

Poet and painter William Blake stated, "**To see a world in a grain of sand - And heaven in a wildflower - Hold infinity in the palm of your hand - And eternity in an hour**". The "seeing" that William Blake is referring to here is not the sight of everyday perception. He is referring to the visionary sight, the making real of something that cannot be counted or held yet.

Unless you have been beamed up by Scotty for the past decade and just got back, you will have heard or seen the phrase "Vision Board". Many authors like Jack Canfield and Rhonda Byrne have praised this method of using the Law of Attraction to bring to you the things you want in our lives. A vision board is a compilation of photos, words, affirmations, and other visual stimulation that represent one's dreams and aspirations. A vision board is a very powerful visualization tool that helps give you clarity of your dreams and aspirations, to program, or maybe reprogram our subconscious with positive images and words that provide a visual reminder of the life you want to live, the goals you want to achieve, and the things you want to attract into our lives

In every culture from time immemorial, there have been tools developed by people who have made advancements to teach others, this is how we have progressed and move forward. Because we are all wonderfully different. We are motivated differently - some through poetry (like Maya Angelou), others by sound (Beethoven) and some like me are visually inclined and find it easier to motivate themselves through vision, and for people like me, a vision board is perfect.

Long before William Blake, before the Renaissance painters and sculptors like da Vinci and Michelangelo (just think of his David!), grappled with portraying the better side of our (and their nature) the ancients knew that in order to visualize something, it helped to have a totem or symbol to remind you. Something to help "keep it in your mind". It is speculated that the drawings in caves, done thousands of years ago were perhaps a reminder for the ancients of the spirit world or the route that the bison would take. The ancients also used a visual aid to help them remember what was important to them.

In today's time, and with modern technology, we do not use physical items like stones and paintings to help us envision a better future for our families and ourselves. What we use are the tools we have such as photographs, printers, hence now the rise and popularity of vision boards.

We know that athletes are using the power of visualization to help them achieve greater success. They imagine the track, the weather, the crowds, their muscles burning with effort as they strain towards the finish line. However, most important of all, they imagine the feeling of joy, accomplishment, and pride when they do cross over that finish line first. They never just imagine the environment; they also imagine the feeling of success at the end of it. Nobody is going to win a race by thinking about just the environment but neglecting the actual feeling of success. Imagine going through that whole process, and at the end thinking 'I hope I won"?

The Law of Attraction is a simple statement, very simple to understand. However, like many simple concepts, it is not always very easy to implement. Simply put, the Law of Attraction states "like attracts like". An example of this is how we often attract friends that share similar interests and viewpoints to us, share experiences with strangers that reinforce our similar views (think of sports games and political parties) and identify with celebrities or shows that reflect our beliefs and concepts (while we would rather watch home Improvement, someone else might prefer Oprah).

Scientists have investigated the Law of Attraction as well, proved it is not just an abstract concept. There are intriguing scientific investigations that show that the brain regions that involve intention are very closely aligned with the areas in the brain that involve action. Therefore, when you activate that regions in your brain for intention, the areas in your brain that lead to action are also all fired up. The strength your intention will lead you to more action and your vision boards are the perfect tools to help strengthen your intention, in order for you to be motivated and act.

A vision board is a visualization tool used to depict our dreams and aspirations, and to reprogram our brain, by reminding it visually, what we could experience in the future. Just like athletes understand that they are going to have to train, and will not win just by wishing it, we understand that vision boards are a tool to help us train, to teach how to hold a mental image in our brain of the things we want to achieve. A vision board is not a wishing board – you cannot just wish your dreams into reality and most intelligent people will agree on that. This is the difference between wishing and true visualizing. With wishing, you blow out the candle and make a wish. That is the extent of your commitment to your dreams and aspirations. You take no active role in manifesting what you wish to achieve. You cannot cut photos out of books, stick them on a board and then wish them into life. That is what is called magical thinking, and is what distinguishes 5-year old from responsible adults.

You have to believe, trust the process, but most importantly you need to act. By taking action you are becoming a co-creator of the life you want. Your line of thought will usually flow something like this: "I wish I could become a doctor", which becomes "I wonder if I could get a student loan?" It grows into applying to medical schools and studying most nights through to graduation. Your vision board on the wall should be there to encourage and remind you of that goal throughout, while you are applying for loans, studying for exams, while working in a hospital at three in the morning, or when you feel like given up.

However, sometimes after cutting and pasting like a 5-year old in pre-school and almost high on glue, we realize that we are not manifesting our dreams and aspirations, and we wonder: "Why don't my vision board work"? Remember, I said vision boards became a fundamental part of my life in 2009. Through my epic failure at my first vision board, accreditation as a certified vision board coach, and experience teaching on vision boards, I have discovered some very fundamental reasons why people don't manifest what's on their vision board.

Have you ever created a vision board and wondered why your dreams weren't being manifested? Well, I have answers. In this book I share three major reasons why vision boards as a success tool doesn't work for 90% of people who create them. As you read through this book, I encourage to keep your mind open, ponder on these three reasons I offer for your consideration. Please understand that these three reasons are just the most common threads I gleamed through my own personal experience, as well as working with people who have created a vision board. Using a vision board as a success tool is a powerful way to stay focus on your goals, but your mindset plays a major role in the process.

My goal is to help you get out your own way, so you can become the best version of yourself, and create your best life. You were created for greatness, and its time for you to dream BIG. Getting to greatness starts with having a vision for your life. Having a vision for your life is the act and power which gives direction to your life to make your dreams and aspirations a reality. It is important to have vision and purpose because it the driving force to your intentions to be your best, and create your best life.

CHAPTER ONE

SELF LIMITING BELIEFS

Self-limiting beliefs are one of the biggest reasons why vision boards do not work for people. All the books on self-help and religion have emphasized the same point: You can do anything you want. The only way that these books differ is in partnerships with whom. These great thinkers have all realized the one thing that you have to be able to do, which is believe in yourself.

Simple, but not easy!

What is a self-limiting belief? Self-limiting beliefs are assumptions or perceptions that you've got about yourself, your abilities, and about the way you believe the world works. These assumptions are self-limiting because in some way they hinder or hold you back from becoming the best version of yourself, achieving what you are capable of, and creating your best life. Let me give you an example: An elephant, when it is young, is trained in the circus by tying its leg with a very heavy chain, which is tied to a deeply driven stake in the ground. The young elephant will struggle to free himself from this heavy chain, pushing and pulling, but after a while, he will realize that he cannot pull himself free. Once that shift in perception happens, he can now be tied with a very slim rope - simply because his mind has been limited in his belief. This huge animal, with the biggest body on land, will now be controlled with a slight rope – simply because he believes he cannot do it.

In much the same way, when some people believe that they cannot do something, it is very hard to change the way they perceive the world. Once the idea has taken root, been dug in with a deep stake, they also will believe they cannot, or should not, or will fail - and with each thought, they drive the stake deeper into the ground. They never stop to think of what that thought is grounded in. Examples: "Money is the root of all evil", "There isn't enough money to do what I want" or the classic, though very often subconscious "I don't deserve it" are all familiar to us. We are usually vaguely aware when we think about them that they are self-limiting. If we are somewhat conscious of the thought, we try to mitigate it with a softly uttered "but I can". Sometimes, when we are allowing negative thoughts to enter our minds, we are trying to protect ourselves from disappointment and hurt. However, try as you might, that soft whisper will not dig that deep stake out of the ground.

Like the elephant that does not realize it can push over full-grown trees with its strength, you do not realize the strength of your thoughts. When you have limited beliefs about yourself, and your abilities, it causes you to believe that your limitations are more than your ability to achieve. Unconscious, or conscious self-limiting beliefs has the power to sabotage your potential through the actions or non-actions you take based on your beliefs. This is why vision boards don't work for some people. Their self-limiting beliefs are more powerful then the pictures and words on their vision board, so therefore, their conscious mind fool them into believing their vision is unachievable.

How to identify a Limiting Belief

Let us say you have a picture of a beautiful home on your vision board. It is a shingle cottage standing on a beach, curtains swaying with a light ocean breeze, glasses on a table with a view of an azure ocean beyond. You look at the picture and can imagine yourself sitting on your patio enjoying your ocean view, you can feel the breeze against your face, and smell the freshness of the ocean.

Take that thought, or whichever picture you have in your mind, and examine it carefully. What does the ocean remind you of, the table, the curtains blowing? When we look at your vision boards to keep focus on your goals, the mind has a tendency to play tricks on you. You start to get a faintly uneasy feeling after a while that your dreams are beyond your reach. Those limited beliefs lurking in the back of your mind causes you to start doubting and question, what is possible. Those limited beliefs will have you asking yourself these types of thoughts and questions: Perhaps on the beach is not the best place. Should it be in Mauritius rather than the Azores? What if there is a storm surge, would a house like that stand? Would my house be in danger? Would

I have to pay more insurance, and what about privacy – people walking on the beach might invade my privacy and end up having the drinks on my table? Sometimes your thoughts and questions go deeper than that and you just don't believe you can have your dream house. Whenever your thoughts start surfacing you need to investigate. Those are your limiting belief take charge sabotaging your belief of what you can achieve, or become. It is important to identify them, and determine where they are coming from.

Once you can identify the fears and insecurities that are invading your mind things starts to get interesting. You have to start following that belief, as a tracker in the bush, to see where it might lead you because that would be the origin of your belief. Where does that belief come from? From a very early age in childhood, we start to form beliefs about the world and your place in it. And your brain stores these beliefs identifying patterns making associations, so you constantly process the stream of information about the world around you and use it to form beliefs. Generally, the purpose of belief formation is to help you understand the world and stay safe. In early childhood, your beliefs are usually based on your experiences and shaped by your parents or other dominant figures in your lives. As you get older, you start to form more complex self-imposed self-limiting beliefs about yourselves and abilities. Example, seeing someone else failure is much scarier than failing yourself because you witness and experience the anxiety of failure, but ultimately without the pride that you earn once you have overcome that failure. Even when you fail yourself, you still will do anything to protect yourself from that hurt. Instead of using the failure as a lesson, and then letting it go, you allow yourself to be held by it. Unfortunately, most people have been taught that failure is negative and painful, so consequently they don't learn that failure is an important part of life. And because of the pain of failure, your mind will cause you to create limiting beliefs that impact your self-esteem and self-worth.

Nevertheless, the self-limiting beliefs that you form about yourself can be very powerful, and even when you encounter new information or explanations, you often cling to your old beliefs. This is why it is important to identified the root cause of your self-limiting belief. It allows to understand that the slightly uneasy feeling you get when you are trying to manifest your dreams and aspirations. Self-limiting beliefs is one of the biggest reasons why visions boards do not work. We don't realize how much our mind influence the way we are living our lives. It has the power to make us believe in something that often is untrue, and don't serve our well-being. It makes us believe in our limitations more that our abilities to achieve.

Most self-limiting beliefs are subconscious, and it requires a fact-find mission to uncover them, and much reprogramming of your subconscious to change the narrative.

Replacing the Self-Limiting Belief with Limitless Believing

Once you have done the heavy work of identifying your self-limiting beliefs (which is not a simple task) that are stopping you from achieving your goals, you can start to weed them out of your thought processes. For more than half my life I have battled the demon of self-limiting beliefs, are here are a few approaches that was effective with helping me tackle my beliefs:

1. You first have to understand their purpose. I know this sounds crazy, but the point is all beliefs have a purpose, and usually the purpose is to keep you safe or protect you. However, in the case of self-limiting beliefs, the purpose becomes a misguided, and take a life of their own. Earlier I used the example of experiencing failure, our brain will tell us not to take the risk of starting that business because the risk and disappointment can be devasting. The belief is trying to spare you of the pain of rejection, failure, etc. But as I stated, failure is a good teacher that bring forth lesson, even in the disappointment.

2. Questions Them. Once you have identified the purpose of your belief and where it came from, you have to ask the question is it perceived threat real. When I was in the seventh grade, I took a scholastic test that stated I would never be anything more than a cafeteria worker. For years I carried those words like a badge of horror, turning them into a self-fulfilling prophecy. Then one day I had to ask myself was that true? After looking over my life, I realize that there was

no evidence to support the assumption. I was the one who watered the seed, and caused it to bloom to my detriment.

3. Create new beliefs. To break the power of your old beliefs, you need to replace them with new ones that speak to who you really are, and what you can achieve. A self-assessment of what you have accomplished is a great way to change your old beliefs. When you identify all the positive things you have achieved, you can use that to create your new belief. Example, instead of saying you are a victim, you can change that narrative to I AM survivor, conquer, strong, resourceful, or overcomer.

4. Retrain Your Brain. The subconscious needs to be reprogramming from those old narrative into the new ones. Because beliefs are patterns that the brain has identified, feeding it new patterns can start to rewire it. Affirmations are a powerful way of rewiring your brain. Speaking positive affirmation and declarations repeatedly daily feeds your subconscious new information

tricking your conscious mind to believe something different.

These are just a few ways to start replacing your self-limiting beliefs with new ones. I mentioned affirmations are a wonderful tool, but there is also a danger present in them. To look at a picture and say "I will live there on that beach" fifteen times a day is useful, but ultimately you have to remember that you cannot trick the universe into believing in you when you do not believe in yourself. You have to put the work in, because only with the work will you be able to believe yourself. You have to create evidence of success. If you battling to find a picture of evidence of success in your own life, which should not be hard – everyone has been successful at something, however small an achievement they think it to be. If you might have worried for weeks about passing your driver's license exam, and eventually after trying three times you did ... That is a small success. Hold onto that feeling! Remember that feeling when you have a picture of your dream car on your vision board and think "Success!"

You can also Investigate and find someone else's life to see the evidence. There are stories of heroes in every culture and in every medium, and finding them is very easy. Look at these stories and absorb the lessons that these people learned. Ernst Shackleton went to Antarctica with a crew full of men and lost his boat when it was crushed by ice. Despite horrific odds, he managed to bring them all home again, struggling over ice and sea, thousands of miles from civilization. Understand that when a human decides to do wonderful things, there is nothing separating you from them. The same tools, the arms and legs, and minds, are available to everyone. It is only in how we use them there is a difference.

Let us say for instance that you have would like to live in Spain, and you have a picture of the famous Holy Family Church in Barcelona, Spain. However, you have always thought that you are not great at learning new languages, never mind Spanish. After examining your self-limiting beliefs, you have learned that the reason you might not be attracting what you wanted is that you are scared of being laughed at speaking Spanish. You have now identified the limiting belief. Now start by making small changes, and build your confidence in yourself from there. Learning to say hello and goodbye in Spanish might be small steps in the larger scheme of things, but it is these small steps that pave the way for the bigger ones. Then allow yourself to feel proud of your accomplishment. Feel the pride and skip a few steps. You have now changed a limiting belief, and you are changing your future. When you celebrate even small achievements, it encourages you to tackle the larger ones.

When you believe that something is real, your body experiences it as a real event. It is unable to tell the difference. That is why it is so dangerous to focus on negativity, as your body releases cortisol to deal with the stress, and a cycle of negativity continues. It has been scientifically proven that rats subjected to continuous stress battle to break out of repetitive behavior. However, when you experience (or even imagine) a positive event, your body release endorphins, and floods your system with these chemicals. You could have the effect without the actual experience, but the effect is much more amplified when you have even a small positive experience to link it to.

If all else fails, try "if"

If you truly find that you cannot replace negative beliefs with positive ones, you can always return to pretending, as you did in pre-school. Pretending will help you to get over the first stages of quieting down the part of your brain that is stuck in the repetitive behavior, and will allow you to take steps in a positive direction.

Using the Spanish example, what would happen if you told the Spanish-speaking bank teller you are trying to learn Spanish, could she help you? Most probably, she would be flattered and help. However, maybe she is thoughtless and forgets or gets irritated, but now you know you have tried once to reach out for someone to speak with, and if you have done it once, you could do it again.

If you want to attract more abundance, send out abundance in your life. Even if you can only spare a tiny amount of money, put it in a homeless person cup and silently bless him, thanking him for giving you the opportunity to attract blessings into your own life. We might not be able to all donate thousands of dollars, but when you have a little and are prepared to share responsibly, you are using the Law of Attraction. With "if", you have started to create a life that mirrors your vision board. Even smiling at a stranger or helping an injured bird is sharing, and those feelings will come back to you. Live abundantly.

However, you have to recognize that "acting as if it was real" is only a temporary tool. Eventually, you will not be able to fool your body or mind. Real confidence and belief are created by actual successes that come from trying repeatedly, especially the small ones that make the big ones easier and more fun, building on your dream block by block. It has even been speculated by scientists that just imagining it might, in fact, become detrimental to your dreams. When you imagine it, and because your mind thinks it is real, you might be less inclined to actually doing something about it.

Once you have identified your self-limiting beliefs you have absorbed and worked them out of your vocabulary and mind, you will find yourself attracting the things that are important to you so much easier. This will make it easier for you to believe that your dreams and aspirations on your vision board are obtainable, because you believe you are worthy of greatness.

CHAPTER TWO

WHAT ARE THE STORIES YOU ARE TELLING YOURSELF – ABOUT YOURSELF

What are the stories you are telling yourself? The stories you tell yourselves will determine your success. The stories you tell yourselves is connected to our beliefs about yourselves. We have the power to rewrite our story if we truly want to achieve happiness and success.

Hundreds of years ago, a traveler came across two men squaring stones in Paris. He asked one of the men, "What are you doing?" The first stonemason replied, "I am squaring a stone." Still curious, the traveler went up to the second stone mason and asked him what he was doing. "I am building a cathedral," replied the second man. This story illustrates the power of being able to re-imagine a new story for yourself. We all have to build a life for ourselves, but we do not all recognize that we also have the ability to write a different story. Both those stonemasons had the choice to create a story out of their daily work, and I am sure you can guess who was the happier at work during the day and felt more fulfilled at the end of it!

We all have stories that we tell ourselves. Before you say: "I don't have a story that I tell myself" ... Check your figurative basement! For years I told myself that I could never be more than a cafeteria worker, because that what I was told my future held for me. While my reality never mirrored that story, it's the story I used to justify all my disappointments and failures in my life. It wasn't until I did my own rewrite and changed the trajectory of my story. When I look back over my life, I realized that limited belief was said to me in the seventh grade, I buried, and resurrected in my adulthood to justify my disappointments and failures. It was the perfect excuse. The stories we tell ourselves are always there, even if not openly acknowledged - they somehow lurk in our sub-consciousness. These dramas hide in the long drawn out tale we tell ourselves when we say, "mechanics always overcharge me", or "I always get lost when traveling to a new city". They are the stories that repeat themselves like an old movie channel in our mind, replaying scene by scene the things that we have experienced, and buying into someone else drama with every reel.

We have to remember that every day; we have the power to create a new story, not just for our whole life, but also for every small event that happens to us. Let us say you have a picture on your vision board of a woman in a power suit to remind you of your new career. When you spill coffee on your suit shirt on your way to an interview you have two options. Your story could be, I knew this job wasn't meant for me, or I never have any good luck, or you could change it to become a comedy, charming your prospective employer. You have the power to change the narrative. You can even turn it into an inspirational story about putting on a sweater over the stain, keeping your chin up and knocking them dead. Even if you do not get that job, the story could become an inspiration to remember that you went ahead with the interview, despite the obstacles, and you learned from it. If the stories you are telling yourself – about yourself if no longer serving you, you have the power to rewrite the story. Rewriting your story is more of a proactive that reactive approach to making real meaningful changes in your life. Rather than accepting or complaining to what life gives you, you can see yourself as the creator of your own story. One of the most powerful ways to rewrite your story is to have a new vision for your life, and depict that vision with pictures and words on your vision board. But in order for you to manifest that new vision you have to believe you are worthy of having and achieving that need new story. It requires faith, and work.

Understand Your Stories

Understanding your stories helps you to re-imagine a better life for yourself and those you love. Every story that you believe about yourself informs your dreams and aspirations and the only person who can change your story into a hero's tale is you! For example, let us say you have a picture of a man with roses on your vision board. Consciously you would like to have a man who is romantic and brings you flowers. Because you are now aware of your subconscious beliefs, you understand that a reason you might not be attracting what you want in a romantic relationship is that eventually, you end up breaking up because he cheats. You know why you chose someone who cheats is because you do not actually believe that someone can really only love you. The story you tell yourself is rooted in the 'all men are cheaters", and for you to attract someone who is faithful, you need to step out of the drama.

As they say, if the story does not have a happy ending – it is not the end yet! Understanding that you have the power to create a happy ending and attract all that you want means rewriting the story to make yourself the hero of your own fairy tale. In this story, you are a woman who understand all men don't cheat, and past experiences, or other people experiences don't determine your ability to attract a healthy relationship absence of infidelity. That is the association that you will make with your vision board – and that is what you will attract into your life. So now, you will be more able to recognize the man that makes you laugh and realizes how awesome you are. You have now re-written your story, and you are waiting for the universe to act out your script.

Tell Yourself a Different Fairy Tale

We are all brought up on rags to riches stories of popular culture, and although we might identify with them on a superficial level, we need to understand that we can also rewrite our own stories that might mirror, or even exceed, their stories. Superficially identifying with these stories might inspire us, but believing yourself to be on the same level will work even better. You have to know that looking at a person in a picture is not the same as identifying with them—you are just observing the outside. Identifying with only their strengths and not their weaknesses is also problematic; it leaves you unable to truly understand that they, like you, have had to overcome struggles to get where they are. We see Brad Pitt with the lovely kids and beautiful wife, and forget about the young Brad in a chicken outfit trying to earn a few bucks, and like us, dreaming of a better life. You can rewrite your stories in so many ways ... When you can rewrite Cinderella story, where instead of waiting for the prince to bring her shoe, she starts a company making glass shoes and meets a successful cobbler. The prince becomes a cobbler, and they live happily ever after, but sometimes still fight about who should do the dishes! When you are able to re-imagine other fairytales, you know you are breaking out of the stories of other people and creating your own destiny.

If you are having a tough day with your boss, remember the story of Snow White and the Evil Queen, and retell it with yourself as the hero. You are Snow White learning to deal with tough people so that eventually, one day, when you are the queen of the land – and you will remember to be patient and understanding, no matter how unpleasant the person you are dealing with is. That is what the picture of the man in a power suit should remind you of.

The reason these old folk tales are still so popular and have lasted throughout the centuries is that humans have always been able to identify themselves in them. That is why they were told repeatedly, for children to be able to see themselves in them and overcome the Evil Queen, or whatever would wait for them into the future. Most of these children could not read, and this was an easy way to teach them lessons about overcoming whatever life might throw at them. Having said that, two hundred years ago, there were very few female entrepreneurs, and most women would only be able to become wealthy, or a princess, with the help of a man. Luckily, that is no longer true! Therefore, you can rewrite the story in whichever way it suits you; your imagination is your best friend!

Getting the Help, You Need

If you look carefully in these stories, you do not have to be alone dealing with the tales of unfulfilled dreams, abandonment and pain. You can re-imagine them to have people (like the Seven Dwarfs for Snow White or the fairies in Sleeping Beauty) who will be ready to help you overcome any obstacle and face all your adversaries. How often have we listened to these stories, but never realized the help the Universe send to us in following our dreams. When you look at the tale of Snow White, we often do not understand that had it not been for unlikely accomplices called Grumpy and Sneezy, the tale might have ended with Snow White being eaten by the Big Bad Wolf instead of becoming a queen.

There are often people around us, standing there clapping for us on the sidelines, whom we do not recognize because we could not imagine them having a part in our story. We are so conditioned by the marketing around us, we do not see the surprising help that is out there right in front of us if we could only recognize it. On the other hand, if we do, we do not appreciate that it might not be the famous celebrity, but is instead the tireless accountant helping us become what we dream of becoming.

When Oprah Winfrey was already successful in the US and wondering how to continue growing her career, she tells of the lawyer that told her to bet on herself, own her brand and have her own syndicated show. Today she says that that bet has paid off much more than even she can realize. It was not just the guru; it was also a good lawyer. Surround yourself with good people that can help you reach your dreams.

Surround Yourself with Equals

All around us are stories that in many ways mirror our own. Maybe not with the same intensity, but stories about people overcoming obstacles. Read about these stories, watch their movies, and learn to identify these people. Ernst Shackleton organized a trip to the Antarctic in 1914 and was a national hero in England on his return in 1917. However, he first had to arrange financing, find out about the weather, get a ship, hire men, navigate and provide for all of the crew. By then he had already attempted to be a journalist, banker, and politician previously, and I am sure people were watching him with raised eyebrows. Still, he decided he wanted to be an adventurer and travel across Antarctica from sea to sea. His story might be different to yours in the details - you are trying to begin fulfilling your dream of having your own bakery, but on many levels, it your story could also be a grand tale of overcoming obstacles and learning all the time.

Read about courageous people, people who wrote their own stories, and surround yourself with them. If someone like Ernst Shackleton inspires you, perhaps you could put up a picture of an old-fashioned sailing boat to represent the strengths you have overcome, and to represent the adventures you will have in a new life that awaits you. These images and stories will help you to remember that you can write a different story and be a hero too.

Knowing our story is important when creating a vision board, or trying to create any type of success because it speaks to what your conscious mind believe about you. Are the stories you telling yourself, or believe about yourself true. Is your conscious mind telling your subconscious that you can't have the dreams and aspirations you have reflected on your vision board?

CHAPTER THREE

NEVER WISH HARDER THAN YOU ARE PREPARED TO WORK

> *Dreams without goals and action are just dreams deferred.*

You can ask God for what you want, but if you are not willing to work for your dreams, they won't magically happen. A vision board is a visual tool used to motivate and keep your dreams and goals in the forefront of your mind. If you don't set goals, and take action towards your goals, manifesting the things on your vision board will not work.

We have all often read about vision boards, where we come across a story about how a woman met her future husband moments after pinning her vision board to the wall, the glue not even dry yet. Alternatively, somebody won the lottery just after sticking a picture of gold bars on her vision board. While these things can certainly happen, we must remember that it is seldom that the Universe throws gold coins in our piggy banks - no one would ever grow emotionally or spiritually stronger that way. This might be why so many people completely lose their bearings after winning a lot of money because they did not work for it, they do not appreciate it. People always take the advice they paid for a lot more seriously than advice they did not.

We have to remember that we need to co-create with God. Michelangelo spent three years creating his famous sculpture, David. He lay on his back for 4 years painting the Sistine Chapel. We only shortly stop to think how he must have felt lying on his back painting for all those years. Today, 500 years later he is still famous for having had the tenacity of doing so. Creating takes a lot of time and work when you want to create a new life, so you have to be prepared to take the time and put in the work. Anything worthwhile will take a while time to develop and grow.

Think about something you really enjoy, let us say for example gardening. You spend time in the garden, looking where this plant is happiest or where that plant might need to be pruned. You observe that this plant is in the shade in winter and its battles. You stare at a friend's garden and beg shoots off them and you dream with a coffee in your hand while staring at the antics of the birds in your garden. When you love someone or something, you spend the time necessary to nurture that love. Everything that is important to us is something we spend time on.

Your vision board will not work if you do not spend time pursing the goals associated with your vision board.

Most people put much effort into creating their vision board, but spend little to no time working on flushing out the goals make the vision a reality? This is maybe one of the most important part of our journey, and yet, like entitled children we expect the universe to deliver us exactly what we want when we want it.

But what I tell all my clients is the vision board is a tool, and like faith without work it is dead. I remember being told of a story of a man who wanted to be a computer programmer. He is the eldest of four children, and his mother had been a widow since he was 9 years old. After high school, he did not go to college, he had to get a job. This was the early nineties. He started training as a telephone repair technician and qualified. Then he asked for a transfer to the division that handled data lines – a bit closer to his dream. Him and his coworkers would be working out in the fields regularly and would need to go into the office at night. They would bring VHS movies to watch while the field technicians went out to the line and they were waiting for feedback. However, because at work he had access to the best computers of the time, he would practice his programming skills. I do not need to tell you now that he is a well-paid programmer. He was successful because instead of watching an Eddie Murphy movie that he would soon forget. He spent his time making his dreams real. Self-limiting beliefs and the stories we tell ourselves play a key role in our success. But the one of the biggest reasons why people never manifest their dreams and aspiration is because they don't do the work. You can create the most beautiful vision boards, with the perfect pictures and most profound words and affirmations, but if you take no action towards your goals, it was just a wasted exercise.

Take the Small First Steps

The first step to co-creating with the Universe and applying the Law of Attraction is making your Vision board. Nevertheless, you have to remember, this is your first step. Then you have to take small steps to make it real.

After you have pasted the picture of the Eiffel Tower on your board, do not just stand back and wait with your hands in your pockets. Start saving for the trip to France by having a small coin jar on your kitchen counter marked "Saving money for France trip". Enter those competitions where you might win a trip to France. You could find out about loyalty schemes that might increase your air miles. Hustle, and do what you can to help the universe bring what you desire closer.

This will also apply if you want to start your own business. Put up the image of a skyscraper on your board, phone that friend that started their own business;

find out what pitfalls and opportunities there might be. Put your name on an e-mail list for a new job. Save your pizza money for a new computer.

Working towards your vision need not be in big steps – perhaps you could look on the internet who might be able to sell your product? Are there any other beekeepers in your area for when you want to start your own honey making business? Where do they get their bottles? These are all very small steps, some things that could be accomplished in an afternoon, but you are working with the universe towards what you want, and every little step you take brings your goal two steps closer because the universe is co-creating with you.

When you do many small things, eventually it builds up like a puzzle, and if you look carefully, you can see your vision emerging. Therefore, the picture of the Eiffel tower leads to pocket money for the trip, and the loyalty points on your card bring the dream even closer. Before you know it, you will be standing in the check-in, on your way back home after your dream holiday.

Being Scared of Failing

We are all scared of failure, though successful people are usually much too busy to think about it a lot. Not many people have been thankful for failure, except for a few very wise exceptions. However, we have to remember: "The greater the obstacle, the more glory in overcoming it". When you hear those clichés about overcoming failure, you realize that every successful person has had to scrap an idea and move on to another, often over and over. They might have thought this wonderful idea the previous night how a light bulb might work, sure that it was definitely going to overcome a problem they were having like in Edison's famous experience. However, in the light of day, it did not happen hundreds of times. However, the next moment they were thinking of something else that might work - they did no t think of them as failures. Those were just ideas that did not work at that moment. Successful people do not take the failure personally; they just keep chipping away at the mountain, but maybe just with a different hammer.

Michelangelo did not start with David. He did not start with big bold sculptures. He started with small plaques and tried to do them perfectly – he worked on the small things, then bigger sculptures until eventually when the big sculptures were appointed to him and he was ready and able to build on his experiences and co-create with the Universe.

The marble block he was given to carve for David was seriously flawed, so much so that many sculptors of the time said it was impossible to work with. Michelangelo drew for months to incorporate that flaw into his design before he picked up a chisel. Even with all that planning, David still took him three years to carve, one blow with a hammer at a time. He would work at night with candles in a hat, wax dripping on his eyebrows, during the freezing winters and boiling summers. However, when it was finished, it was acknowledged as one of the finest sculptures in Italy. Moreover, the Italians were a very tough crowd to please!

I am sure just like us with our vision boards, after drawing that block for months Michelangelo could feel every curve in the marble block, where there were veins and how it felt when the sun shone on it. He must have been able to visualize that sculpture perfectly, but only after, he spent the time designing, planning and working on it. By then he must have been so familiar with it, failure was no longer an option. He could not do anything but carve the most beautiful sculpture in Italy. If he thought about failing, and I am very sure he did (he was human after all), he must have just tried a different strategy, because he knew he would succeed.

Remove Toxicity

You should avoid toxic people as much as possible while you are building your dreams. If you are a slightly self-disciplined person, you know it is very hard to control your own behavior, and it is almost impossible to control other people behaviors. Do not even try. The first important lesson is to know which is the friend whom you could tell all your dreams too. Identify the people who love the negativity, and when you find them, run – do not walk – in the opposite direction!

One of the most important skills you will have to learn is to differentiate between a toxic person and a realistic person. A realistic person will also point out dangers and pitfalls to you, which is why there are so many lawyers and accountants. However, unlike a toxic person, they will have suggestions on how they think you could avoid the problem. You need real people around you; otherwise, you might be in danger of not seeing boulders falling towards you because you are focused on getting the stone out of your shoe.

However, toxic people are a different matter altogether. You will always recognize a toxic person because they are the ones who will try to impress you with their cynicism, telling you how things can go wrong with no suggestion on how to make your plans work. Remember it is always easier to find something wrong with an idea that it is to find something right. These people are too lazy or scared to look for the good in any idea or situation, but they will hide their laziness and fear by trying to warn you of something, or tell you why you cannot, rather than why you can.

Unfortunately, sometimes you cannot run away, especially if they are family or friends. If you have to deal with someone like this, have a stock answer at hand for when they start their negativity. Perhaps you could just respond with a neutral "Is that so?" A neutral phrase will stop you from becoming entangled in other people's small dramas. It will act as a reminder to you that you are about to enter dangerous territory. You have to try to change the subject as soon as you can. I hope that sooner rather than later, they will have forgotten their dramas.

You are working hard to actualize your dreams, do not let toxic people break it down. When you allow toxic people to poison you, you are giving them permission to break down your dreams. Never try to correct them either, because that will just become an argument and you will only have more toxic waste to clean up after someone charges out of the room. The Law of Attraction will always work here too: If you put negative energy out there – negative energy will come back to you.

Treat your dreams as if you would treat a small child growing up. Encourage your dreams and protect them, because while you are still envisioning, they are very fragile. Handle them with care. A good saying to always remember is "The person saying it cannot be done, should stop interrupting the person doing it!"

Sometimes you might not be sure if someone is toxic or realistic, and for those situations, it is best to have a solution at hand. When you are not sure, I think the best advice to remember was written more than a hundred years ago and is the first lines of the famous poem from Rudyard Kipling, called "If".

In the opening stanza of this much love poem, Kipling warns his readers to be prepared to face toxic people and urges them to keep their head and trust themselves. However, he makes a very important distinction as well, one, which is often overlooked. This distinction is to "make allowance for their doubting too". So, the man e-mailing from Nigeria promising you millions (with which you are going to start your new business) if you just send a couple of thousand to him, most probably deserves to be investigated a bit more. Run – do not walk – away fast! Always keep an open mind, but not so open that your brain falls out!

The first four lines of 'IF', by Rudyard Kipling are always worth memorizing for when you are dealing with negative feedback actually the whole poem is worth memorizing):

> If you can keep your head when all about you
> Are losing theirs and blaming it on you,
> If you can trust yourself when all men doubt you,
> But make allowance for their doubting too

Enthusiasm

The Oxford Dictionary defines enthusiasm as "Intense and eager enjoyment, interest, or approval". It comes from the early 17th-century French *enthousiasme* or via late Latin from Greek *enthousiasmos*, from *enthous* 'possessed by a god, inspired' (based on *Theos* 'God'). Enthusiasm calls to mind "loving what you are doing", it is very hard to stay enthusiastic when you are not loving being in the present moment.

Ralph Waldo Emerson said, "Nothing great has ever been achieved without enthusiasm." When you are doing something with enthusiasm, you are not conscious of much else except that what you are doing. Time fly's past and you catch yourself being totally in the present moment, with no thoughts other than the issue at hand. You become absorbed by it, and the creative movement of the Universe will carry you forward without too much thinking on your part.

When you add something to your vision board, make sure to only add things that you can find yourself being enthusiastic about. It is one of the quickest ways to distinguish if you are aiming for grandiosity or greatness. It is worth repeating: Do not invest your time and energy on something that you cannot enthusiastically carry in your mind. You have to love thinking about it, love talking about it and love working on it. If you are not truly enthusiastic, it becomes too hard for you to live like that. If you are acting without enthusiasm, you are by definition "uninspired".

Leave blank spaces

Let us say you have assembled all your pictures for your board. You have had fun with the process of designing and creating your board and cannot wait to get it up on the wall. The sun on the beach is looking inviting, and you cannot wait to feel the sand between your toes. However, there is one last thing to remember ...

Always leave black spaces on your board. Intentionally.

Just as if meditation is the silence between thoughts, energy can only really flow when there is an open area for it to flow into. Meditation is not visualizing, it is the absence of thought. That is why it is people are so peaceful when they have finished meditating – because they have experienced the absence of what has been called "the chattering monkey of the mind".

It might look impressive to you that you have many dreams with a packed board, but just like too much stuff in your house feels oppressing, too much stuff on your board can become distracting and disabling. Do I have to focus on the sea or mountains …? Should we go to Paris or Amsterdam first? Do you see how your mind becomes cluttered? You must try to never do that to yourself.

If you cannot decide on one place to go to, find an as accurate as possible representation of what you want to do. Do you want to go to the Middle East? Then might it not be better to have one picture than to have a hundred pictures of the Pyramids, and the Nile, and the Wailing Wall and the Dead Sea all cluttering up space on your board? Distill your pictures until you can find the one that is your dream, in its purest form. You should always remember that your pictures should help you keep focused on your dream – it is the entire point of having the Vision Board.

Leave space open intentionally … The point with leaving a space intentionally is that you acknowledge that the Universe will sometimes bring things into your life that you do not have the capacity yet to even dream of. It keeps you always alert to the possibilities you might not even suspect are around you.

God has bigger dreams for us than we can ever imagine, and when you leave some space open, you are intentionally inviting Him to help you play.

Finally, …

Your vision board must be a representation of the things that you are, and the person that you want to be. When you look at a small little acorn, that little acorn has no other picture in its genetics than to become a mighty oak. That is the only thing that the little acorn will aspire to. It is programmed to go from acorn to sapling, to towering oak. There is no doubt within itself about maybe becoming a willow or an elm…? The future mighty oak is pulling that tiny acorn to itself. All it needs to know about being a mighty oak is already in it, it now only needs to grow into its own greatness.

Keep your vision somewhere you can see it often, for instance at your desk or before you go to bed on your bedside table. You need to see it often because that will help you stay focused to make that phone call instead of surfing the web, or to remind you that you still need to look for the cheaper flights to France. As the old saying goes:" Out of sight is out of mind!"

Your vision board should never become a static piece of art; you should try to always let it evolve with you. To come back to the little acorn, it does not stay an acorn forever. It evolves and grows, and so should you. When you have a picture on the board that no longer feels right, change it. Do not bind yourself to something you cannot be completely committed tos. Just like dating, a man that is not right for you stops you from looking for someone who is, it will only limit you. Take it down, change your dream!

When you were a little kid, one of your dreams might have been to drive a car as your dad did. You eventually learned how to drive, so your dream changed. Sometimes our dreams change for other reasons or circumstances beyond our control, but we are too scared to acknowledge it in case we appear to others as indecisive. Acknowledging that we have changed helps us to stay focused on what we are becoming, instead of halfheartedly wasting energy on something we no longer really want to do.

Acknowledging change is not indecisive, it truly knows yourself. All the great minds in history have taught us that knowing yourself is one of the best things we can do for ourselves in this lifetime. This is the wisdom that age often brings, but we do not have to age to know it, and one of the most important things we learn as we build our vision boards. Older people are often seen as eccentric because they know themselves well enough not to be distracted by the expectations of society. If they do not like soy sausages, they are not going to pretend that they do in order to impress anybody else!

Your vision board is the tool you decided to use to get close and intimate with your dreams, to reprogram your subconscious mind to see what you desire and want, to bring goals to your dreams, visualize your future, and to grow personally and professionally.

At its best a vision board, it is the tool we use to remind us of the greatness we are destined to achieve.

The above are the top three biggest obstacles that I have identified that keep people from achieving success with their vision board. Your belief determines what you manifest, so if you don't believe in yourself, your capabilities, or worth, a vision will not change that. A vision board is a pictorial representation of your dreams and aspirations that you believe you can achieve, and deserve.

It is time to pull out your old vision board or create a new one with a renewed sense of what you need to manifest your dreams. The above factors referenced go beyond creating a vision board. Your happiness, peace, and success are tied into goes beyond your vision board, it extends to self, and some of the barriers mentioned in this e-book.

If you would like to about other mistakes that keep your vision board for from working, you can visit us at www.tawawn.com.

ABOUT THE AUTHOR

An Amazon bestselling author, Certified Personal and Executive Coach, and one out of 250 Certified Vision Board Coaches/Instructors who has served clients nationwide, and provided personal development for government, non-profit and the private sector. Tawawn has written several books to include: Stop Hiding Behind Yourself – The Seven Principles to Exposing the Hidden You and Discovery Your Sparkle Effect, Get Your Power – 6 Steps to Take Charge of Your Life, and a host of other books. She is the founder of the Achieve Big Now Academy and the Movement Women Walking in Their Own Shoes. Her mission is simple, and that is to help organizations and individuals maximize their potential and achieve success.

Tawawn believes vision boards are one of the most powerful visualization success tools you can use to help manifest the success you desire. Tawawn has been using vision boards for over 7+ years, and have incorporated the concepts and principles into her corporate and individual coaching and mentoring program.

If you don't have a vision, Tawawn challenges you to create your vision board today, and to use it as inspiration and motivation as you work towards your goals and aspirations.

If you have a vision board, and you are not manifesting your dreams and goals, Tawawn encourages you to read this book again, and figure out why your vision board is not working.

If you would like Tawawn to consult with you on your current vision board, or would like to attend one of her EnVision Your Future – The Vision Board Experience Masterclass, please visit her at www.tawawn.com.

If you would like to learn more about Tawawn, her programs, products and services, please visit us at www.tawawn.com.

www.ingramcontent.com/pod-product-compliance
Lightning Source LLC
Chambersburg PA
CBHW052030290426
44112CB00014B/2449